The Illustrated War Reports

The Great War At Sea

The Opening Salvos

Contemporary Combat Images
from the Great War

First published in this format in Great Britain in 2015 by
Pen & Sword Military
An imprint of
Pen & Sword Books Ltd
47 Church Street
Barnsley
South Yorkshire
S70 2AS

ISBN 9781473837867

Printed and bound in Malta
By Gutenberg Press Ltd.

Pen & Sword Books Ltd incorporates the Imprints of Aviation, Atlas,
Family History, Fiction, Maritime, Military, Discovery, Politics, History,
Archaeology, Select, Wharncliffe Local History, Wharncliffe True Crime,
Military Classics, Wharncliffe Transport, Leo Cooper, The Praetorian Press,
Remember When, Seaforth Publishing and Frontline Publishing.

For a complete list of Pen & Sword titles please contact
PEN & SWORD BOOKS LIMITED
47 Church Street, Barnsley, South Yorkshire, S70 2AS, England
E-mail: enquiries@pen-and-sword.co.uk
Website: www.pen-and-sword.co.uk

Contents

An Introduction to the series 4

Chapter 1 The naval arms race 14

Chapter 2 The war in the North Sea 56

Chapter 3 The war extends 72

An introduction to the series

The photographic equipment in use during the Great War was cumbersome and bulky and the environment of the trenches was highly lethal. As a result, the ability to take snapshots was extremely limited, making it all but impossible to capture meaningful shots of the fleeting moments of action. Furthermore the output of cameramen was subject to intense censorship; in consequence, action sequences from the front were so rare and sanitised that the popular magazines reporting the events, on both sides of the line, were forced to recruit artists and illustrators to fill the gap.

These artists were called upon to produce a highly accurate visual record of the events the camera could not capture; hand to hand fighting, trench raids, aerial dogfights, sea battles, desperate last stands, individual acts of heroism, night actions and cavalry charges. They were there to record events on the battlefield for commercial purposes and their work usually found a home in popular magazines such as *The War Illustrated*. The result of their efforts was a huge body of work which spanned the full gamut of styles ranging from the simplest of sketches through to highly finished oil paintings on a grand scale.

In their foremost ranks were skilled technicians such as Richard Caton-Woodville Jr. and William Barnes Wollen both of whom can stand comparison with the great artists of any age. Many of these artists including, of course, Richard Caton-Woodville Jr. had served in the military. They were amazingly talented and their work is of superb quality. They also had the eye for detail in terms of uniform, equipment and weapons which brings added authenticity to their work. They were also able to conjure up for the viewer an impression of the genuine stresses and strains of combat from the soldier's point of view.

The Second Battle of Ypres by Barnes Wollen

The canon of works by these two great artists alone includes such masterpieces as Barnes Wollen's Landrecies, 25 August 1914, The Defeat of the Prussian Guard, Ypres, 1914, The Canadians at Ypres and The London Territorials at Poziers. Richard Caton-Woodville Jr.'s works include The Piper of Loos, The Battle of the Somme, The 2nd Batt. Manchester Regiment taking Six Guns at dawn near St. Quentin, The Entry of the 5th Lancers into Mons, The Charge of the 9th Lancers at Moncel, 7 September 1914, and the magnificent Halloween, 1914: Stand of the London Scottish on Messines Ridge.

The charge of the 9th Lancers at a German battery near Mons by Richard Caton Woodville Jr.

It is a strange state of affairs but even with such luminaries to call upon, the work of the contemporary combat illustrators of the Great War, for illustrative purposes, is today almost entirely overlooked in favour of the work of the photographers.

The reason for this sad state of affairs lies in the fact that, besides the excellent work by the likes of the brilliant Barnes Wollen, there was an army of more pedestrian artists at work and many of the lesser gifted were engaged in turning out crude images to feed the populist pages of the consumer publishing machine. Primarily as a result of their efforts the whole corpus of wartime illustration has become tainted with the tag of propaganda, and in consequence the remarkable work of even the greatest of Great War graphic artists is now extremely unfashionable. It is considered to be vulgar and is routinely dismissed as melodramatic and jingoistic and all too often mischaracterised simply as crude populist propaganda. Publishers now turn their backs on these works which are no longer considered worthy to illustrate modern history books.

Things That Matter. Colonel Fitz-Shrapnel receives the following message from G.H.Q. "Please let us know, as soon as possible, the number of tins of raspberry jam issued to you last Friday."

Another group at work in the trenches were the humorists and chief among those was the peerless Bruce Bairnsfather. Bairnsfather had seen action during 1914 and 1915 as a

The Kensingtons at Laventie by Eric Kennington

machine gun officer serving with the Warwickshire Regiment. His finely observed work grew out of his experience in the Ypres salient and began to appear in *The Bystander* during 1915. By 1917 Bairnsfather was already one of the most widely recognised artist/illustrators of his day, but in our day his work is viewed as holding little relevance for serious students of the Great War. This is a great shame as his finely crafted observations have a great deal to tell us concerning the appalling conditions endured with such stoicism by the British troops on the Ypres salient serving under the shadow of the German trenches.

Fortunately there remains a wider appreciation for the work of the official war artists. We can be thankful that, in addition to the work of the still photographers and the illustrators, there was a general appreciation by the governments of all sides that, as well as the simple act of recording the events, there was also the need to record that which 'the camera cannot interpret'.

The British government in particular came to the gradual realisation that 'a war so epic in its scope by land, sea and air, and so detailed and complex in its mechanism', required interpretation, not just by technicians, but also by artists and this led to the appointment of the first official war artists. The War Artists were able to present a vivid picture of the world as it really was, in full colour, just like our own world and today, through their work we are privileged to have access to a remarkable record of the Great War which brings back the dimension of colour to an otherwise grey world.

The British official war artists were a select group of artists who were employed on contract, or commissioned to produce specific works during the Great War. However it wasn't until May 1916, some two years after the outbreak of the war, that the British Government appointed Muirhead Bone as Britain's first official war artist.

Official war artists were appointed by governments to record events as a matter of record but others were commissioned for propaganda purposes. War artists depicted diverse aspects of the

Ready to start by William Orpen

Great War through his or her art; this might be a pictorial record or a comment on some other aspect of war or it might seek to cast a light on how war blights lives. Muirhead Bone worked exclusively in pencil and ink with publication in Government magazines in mind. As a result, through his work, we still see the world in the same monochrome shades as the official photographs.

However, after Bone returned to England, he was replaced by his brother-in-law Francis Dodd. It is disappointing that Dodd specialised mainly in portraits many of which could just as easily have been created at home. They throw little light on the nature of the Great War. In addition Dodd was very sparing in his use of colour, but the muted red shades which occasionally creep into his work indicated that the door to the world of colour was at last sliding open. Mercifully, in 1917, arrangements were made to send other artists who possessed greater artistic ambition to France. Included in their ranks was Eric Kennington who is best known for his painting of 'The Kensingtons at Laventie' which depicted his former unit at rest during a lull in the hard-fought battles of 1915. Although there were no official war artists before 1916, Kennington had already served at the front with the 13th Battalion of The London Regiment who were known as 'The Kensingtons', he saw action from 1914 until he was invalided out in June 1915 after accidentally shooting himself in the toe!

The famous painting was constructed from memory and depicts the artist in 1915 standing behind and to the right of the soldier in the white hat. Kennington recreates the scene as his platoon rested in a village after four sleepless days and nights in the snow covered trenches. The exhausted men are waiting for the order to march on to

1st Artist Rifles by Paul Nash

a warm billet and the picture conveys that sense of almost dreamlike weariness. With Kennington we at last begin to experience the world of the Great War, not as a hum drum monochrome but as a world of emotion and colour. It was also the beginning of a trend which was to lead to a remarkable body of work as artists on both sides worked to capture the essence of the events as they saw them.

William Orpen was another official war painter who was able to open a door to the events of the Great War. In 1917 he travelled to the Western Front and along with the usual official portraits of generals and politicians he produced drawings and paintings of private soldiers, dead soldiers and German prisoners of war. His self portrait ' Ready To Start' depicts the artist reflected in a mirror while preparing to set off for duty in the Front Line and neatly encapsulates the manner on which war intrudes on the ordinary world.

For his war work, Orpen was made a Knight Commander of the Order of the British Empire. He was selected as a member of the Royal Academy in 1919. Orpen gave most of his war time works, some 138 in all, to the British government on the understanding that they should be framed in simple white frames and kept together as a single body of work. They are now in the collection of the Imperial War Museum in London. William Orpen came to loathe the politicians who prolonged the Great War but he also relied upon them for post-war commissions so he chose to embody his subtle criticism in his work.

Orpen produced some very strong work during the war, but interestingly he was also present at the political wrangling after the war. His large paintings of the Versailles Peace Conference feature a rather insolent focus on the gilt trappings of the room rather than the politicians gathered there. There is an emphasis on distortion. By doing that he made a strong statement concerning the distorted nature of the political wranglings and the insignificance of the politicians compared to framework which was built on the sufferings of those who made the golden prospects of peace possible.

Even more outspoken was the artist who, like Orpen, witnessed the events in France, he was Paul Nash. The young Paul Nash reluctantly enlisted in the Artists' Rifles and was sent to the Western Front in February 1917 by which time he was a second lieutenant in the Hampshire Regiment. A few days before the Third Ypres offensive he fell into a trench, broke a rib and was invalided home. While recuperating in London, Nash worked from his front-line sketches to produce a series of works which accentuated the harshness of the war. His work such as the celebrated paintings Over The Top (the 1st Artist Rifles at Marcoing), the Menin Road and the Ypres Salient at Night embodies the influence of the Vorticist movement, in fact it became the vanguard of that movement and was well received when it was exhibited later that year at the Goupil Gallery. His work was also featured in *Blast* magazine.

The staff of the Propaganda bureau were naturally wary of the anti-war sympathies which were embodied in the work of Paul Nash and they subjected the artist to particularly strict control. Nash objected to such censorship and he recorded his views in a letter home to his wife dated 16th November 1916 in which he wrote, 'I am no longer an artist interested and curious, I am a messenger who will bring back word from the men who are fighting to those who want the war to go on for ever. Feeble, inarticulate, will be my message, but it will have a bitter truth, and may it burn their lousy souls.'

The story of the men who fought in the Great War was tough and brutal, but even worse was the experience of those who were maimed by shellfire or poisoned by gas. The artist who was best positioned to highlight their plight was Christopher R. W. Nevinson.

At the outbreak of the war Nevinson joined the Friends' Ambulance Unit, which his father had helped to found, and was deeply disturbed by his work tending wounded French soldiers. For a brief period he served as an ambulance volunteer, in 1915, ill health forced his return to Britain.

Nevinson used these experiences as the subject matter for a series of powerful paintings which used Futurist techniques to great effect. His 1916 painting of French Troops Resting is a perfect example of how the modernist style could be harnessed to capture the misery of even day to day life in the war. Nevinson's painting 'La Mitrailleuse' tells us everything we need to know about the industrial nature of the war and Walter Sickert wrote 'this will probably remain the most authoritative and concentrated utterance on the war in the history of painting'.

Nevinson volunteered for home service with the Royal Army Medical Corps, before being invalided out; he was eventually appointed as an official war artist, though his later paintings, based on a short visit to the Western Front, lacked the same powerful reception as those earlier works which had helped to make him one of the most famous young artists working in England. The reason for the loss of impact lies in the fact that, by 1917, Nevinson was no longer finding Modernist styles adequate for describing the horrors of modern war and he switched to a realistic style. 'Paths of Glory' depicts

Gassed by John Singer Sargeant

two fallen British soldiers in a never ending landscape of mud and barbed wire, this particular study is typical of his later war paintings. It is starkly realistic and it's notable for the complete lack of Futurist or Vorticist effects. Similarly, 'A Taube' reflects the human cost of an air raid. We expect to see a Taube, which was a German aircraft, but by juxtaposing the name of the aircraft with the pathetic, lifeless body of a child, Nevinson achieves a far greater effect.

The Great War was fought not just on land, but at sea and in the air. Every bit as important as all of these theatres was the home front where superhuman efforts were required to keep the armed forces in weapons, rations and ammunition. These were the sinews of war and John Lavery was the artist who was recruited to paint pictures of the home front. In this industrial war, what happened at home was every bit as important as the events on the fighting fronts. Without arms, ammunition and the whole paraphernalia that an army needs, everything just grinds to a halt. The labour shortage transformed society by bringing women into the war effort and he did a wonderful job of depicting the effects of the war on the home front. However, we should not overlook the contribution of other outstanding artists working in the same field such a Walter Bayes

who painted the famous image of families taking shelter in the underground.

It's here on the home front that we see female artists at work and artists such as Anna Airy and Flora Lion did a remarkable job of capturing those images of women at work in what had previously been a man's world. The fact that women were not just doing the work but also making the art was a double departure from the norm.

A war artist essentially creates a visual account of war by showing its impact as men and women are shown waiting, preparing, fighting, working, suffering and celebrating. The works produced by war artists are immensely varied and they form an all too often overlooked record of many aspects of war. They record differing aspects of individual's experience of war, whether allied or enemy, service or civilian, military or political, social or cultural.

Perhaps the most famous painting to emerge from the Great War is Gassed by John Singer Sargeant, it depicts the aftermath of a mustard gas attack on the Western Front in August 1918. In the painting, a line of British soldiers who have been exposed to a gas attack are being led along a duckboard walkway at le Bac-du-sud dressing station by a medical orderly. Their eyes are bandaged as a result of exposure to gas and each man holds on to the shoulder of the man in front. There is another line of temporarily

For What? by Frederick Varley

blinded soldiers in the background, and the artist spares the viewer none of the horrors of war as one soldier is leaning over vomiting onto the ground. In contrast to the agony of suffering in the foreground we see a glimpse into the world of those unaffected by the gas as a football match continues in the background, the players oblivious to the horrors of the foreground scene.

Frederick Varley is one of the most justifiably celebrated war artists and his painting entitled 'For What?', captures the desolate futility of the Great War. His study of captured German prisoners is also exceptional. He seems to be saying to us 'well where's the martial glory in all this?' All this effort and expenditure to round up a few ragged individuals who look more like beggars trudging through a ravaged landscape on a road to nowhere. Everything in the painting just screams waste, folly and emptiness.

The German war artists and illustrators were equally hard at work. Without their efforts we wouldn't have the German perspective on unique events such as the war from the perspective of the crew of a Zeppelin over London. Despite the prevailing national stereotype of the humourless Teuton, the Germans too had their satirists. They mainly found expression in the long running Bavarian humour magazine *Simpliccissimus*. The artist who has risen to the highest prominence is, of course, Otto Dix, his 'Stormtroopers Advancing Under Gas', is now one of the most famous images to emerge from the Great War. This work was released as both an etching and an aquatint by Dix in 1924. During this period Dix had begun to specialise in the grim reality of the lingering effects

Stormtroopers Advancing Under Gas by Otto Dix

of the war in Weimar Germany. His images of the war wounded and the decaying moral fabric of German society have a haunting quality which still hits home hard even today. Along with George Grosz, Dix is widely considered one of the most important artists of the Neue Sachlichkeit. When the First World War erupted, Dix enthusiastically volunteered for the German Army. He was assigned to a field artillery regiment in Dresden. In the autumn of 1915 he was assigned as a non-commissioned officer of a machine-gun unit on the Western front and took part in the Battle of the Somme. In November 1917, his unit was transferred to the Eastern front until the end of hostilities with Russia, and in February 1918 he was stationed in Flanders. Back on the western front, he fought in the German Spring Offensive. He earned the Iron Cross (second class) and reached the rank of vizefeldwebel. In August of that year he was wounded in the neck, and shortly after he took pilot training lessons. He was discharged from service in December 1918.

Dix was profoundly affected by the sights of the war, and later described a recurring nightmare in which he crawled through destroyed houses. He represented his traumatic experiences in many subsequent works, including a portfolio of fifty etchings called 'Der Krieg', published in 1924.

As the centenary of the Great War approached, I decided the time had come to undertake a full scale reappraisal not just of the Official War Artists but also of the neglected output of the contemporary combat artists and illustrators of the Great War.

It was soon apparent that far from being mere romantic fantasies these long neglected images are often highly accurate in every detail. Where the artist was present these works form a Primary source of war reportage which is every bit as important as the written word. These works are often a valid and highly authentic secondary record based on eyewitness accounts. The artists at work during the Great War were able to work with the writers who had witnessed the events and often fighting men themselves and they worked to produce a fresh visual account of the action which could not be recorded by any other means. These illustrations are important as they form a valid record of the reality of the fighting as viewed through contemporary eyes. Taken together these works actually form a priceless picture of how the reality of the action at the front was conveyed to contemporary audiences at a time when the events of the war were still unfolding.

Bob Carruthers 2014

Chapter 1

THE NAVAL ARMS RACE

The Great War at sea was the defining chapter in the story of the dreadnought battleship. The dreadnought model was characterised by several large heavily armoured turrets housing equally sized big guns. Generally, British ships had larger guns and were capable of quicker fire than their German counterparts. In contrast, the German ships had far superior optical equipment and range-finding capabilities. As a result of the famous German proficiency in engineering and design, they were much better compartmentalised and therefore able to deal with damage. The Germans also generally had better ammunition handling procedures, deficiencies in which were to have disastrous consequences for the British battlecruisers at Jutland.

During the first decade of the 20th Century naval technology had undergone a rapid series of advances. The introduction of the turbine led to much higher performance, and its more compact size allowed for improved layout. Whereas pre-dreadnought battleships were generally limited to a maximum speed equivalent to 20 mph, modern ships were capable of at least 23 mph, and in the latest British classes, up to 28 mph. The introduction of the gyroscope and centralized fire control (the 'director' as the British called it), led to dramatic improvements in gunnery. Ships built before 1900 generally had effective ranges of perhaps a mile, whereas the first 'new' ships could fight at a distance of five miles, and the most modern designs could engage at ranges of over seven miles.

At the outbreak of the war oil was just being introduced as the main fuel in order to replace the less efficient coalfired engines. Oil produced as much as 40 per cent more energy per volume, extending range and further improving the internal layout of the most modern ships. Another advantage was that oil gave off considerably less smoke, making visual detection more difficult. This was generally mitigated by the small number of ships so equipped, generally operating in concert with coal-fired ships.

Radio was in early use, with naval ships commonly equipped with radio telegraph.

A new class of ship, the battlecruiser, had appeared just before the war. There were two conflicting approaches to design. The British designs were armed like their heavier dreadnought cousins, but deliberately lacked armour in order to save weight and improve speed. The thinking behind this concept was that they would be able to outgun anything smaller than themselves, and run away from anything larger. The German designs, on the other hand, opted to mount slightly smaller main armament (11 or 12 inch guns compared to 12 or 13.5 inch guns in their British rivals). Despite the resulting loss of speed, the German battlecruisers were able to boast relatively heavy armour.

The torpedo boat caused considerable worry for many naval planners. In theory a large number of these inexpensive ships could attack in masses and overwhelm a dreadnought force. This led to the introduction of ships dedicated to keeping them away from the fleets; known initially as torpedo boat destroyers, they became universally known simply as destroyers. Although the mass torpedo boat raid continued to be a possibility, another solution was found in the form of the submarine. The submarine could approach underwater, safe from the guns of both the capital ships and the destroyers (although not for long), and fire a salvo as deadly as a torpedo boat's. Limited range and speed, especially underwater, made these weapons difficult to use tactically.

The U-boat threat in the Channel, although real, was not considered to be a significant worry to the Admiralty because they regarded submarines as almost useless. Even the German high command regarded the U-boat as 'experimental vessels'. Although it was a major artery of the BEF, the Channel was never attacked directly by the High Seas Fleet. Submarines were generally more effective in attacking poorly defended merchant ships than in fighting surface warships, though several small to medium British warships were lost to torpedoes launched from German U-boats. The submarine menace and countermeasures grew apace during the Great War and the earliest forms of sonar were in its infancy by the end of the war.

Naval mines were increasingly developed. Defensive mines along coasts made it much more difficult for capital ships to get close enough to conduct coastal bombardment or support attacks. The first battleship sinking in the war - that of HMS *Audacious* - was the result of her striking a naval mine on 27 October 1914. Suitably placed mines also served to restrict the freedom of movement of submarines.

Maritime aviation was primarily focused on reconnaissance, with the aircraft carrier being developed over the course of the war. Fighter-bomber aircraft capable of lifting only relatively light loads and the torpedo bomber still lay in the future by the time the war ended.

Vice-Admiral Sir John Jellicoe's flagship, *Iron Duke*, being coaled at Sea. Inset: Vice Admiral Jellicoe

Provisioning a warship. The drawing gives a splendid idea of the hugeness of the task of keeping a big warship in fighting trim. It represents the food for the officers and men only. The food for the guns is, of course, another very big item.

Left: Spoiling for a fight. Immediately war was declared the British fleets stole quietly out into the North Sea, eager to try conclusions with the enemy. The German fleet, however, had planned to postpone the great sea fight.

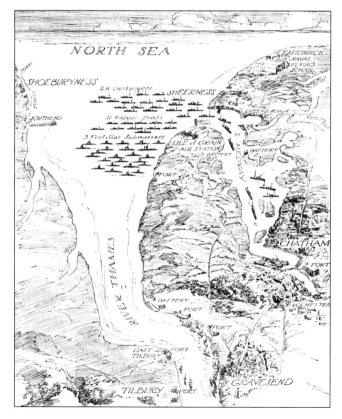

Left: The Estuary of the Thames is very well guarded, as this map shows, and any enemy venturing into it would meet with a hot reception.

Opposite: Guarding the nation's food ships. Every night the Thames estuary bears the above striking appearance. The river is swept constantly with searchlights from British destroyers, and it would go hard with any enemy who attempted to interfere with our freedom of the port.

How our transports were secured from molestation

The Spirit of our old navy yet lives – the 'Drake Touch' in the North Sea.

British torpedo craft displaying exceptional seaworthiness
during a terrific storm in the North Sea.

The German 'High Seas' fleet, which promptly shut
itself up in harbour at the outbreak of War.
The upper portrait is of Admiral von Kœster, and the
lower is that of Admiral von Tirpitz.

Physical sketch map of Wilhelmshaven and district

Working a gun on a German battleship

The *Laertes* – one of the victors in
Heligoland Bight 28 August, 1914.

One of Germany's 240-ton submarines built in 1906

Two British mine layers at work dropping their deadly engines of destruction.

Two British mine-sweepers at the dangerous work of clearing the sea of the German mines, collision with which will send the largest battleship to swift destruction.

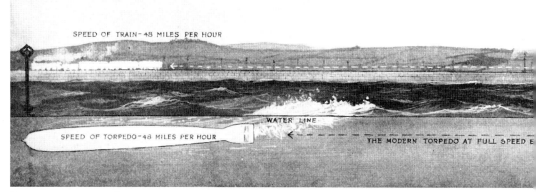

Diagrammatic picture illustrating the discharge and speed of a modern torpedo which travels through the water at the rate of an express train.

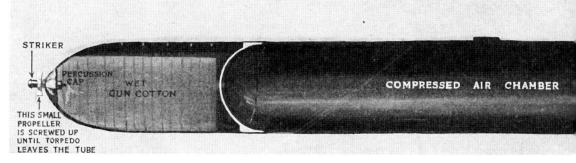

The wonderful mechanism that gives the torpedo its direction and destructive power as a weapon of naval warfare.

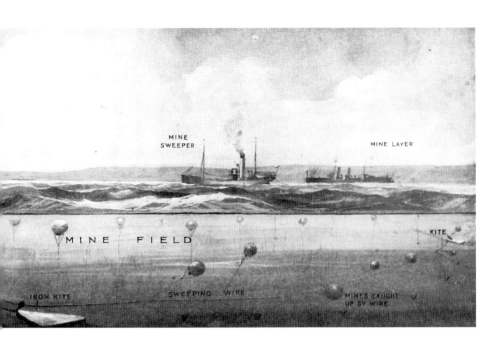

MINE
SWEEPER

MINE LAYER

MINE FIELD

KITE

IRON KITE

SWEEPING WIRE

MINES CAUGHT
UP BY WIRE

FAST TRAIN TRAVELLING
48 MILES PER HOUR

DESTROYER FIRING
TORPEDO

OF A FAST TRAIN

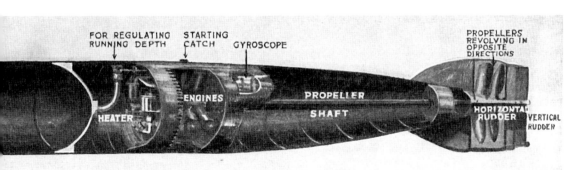

FOR REGULATING
RUNNING DEPTH

STARTING
CATCH

GYROSCOPE

PROPELLERS
REVOLVING IN
OPPOSITE
DIRECTIONS

HEATER

ENGINES

PROPELLER

SHAFT

HORIZONTAL
RUDDER

VERTICAL
RUDDER

British mine sweepers at their hazardous work clearing
the seas of mines laid by Germans.

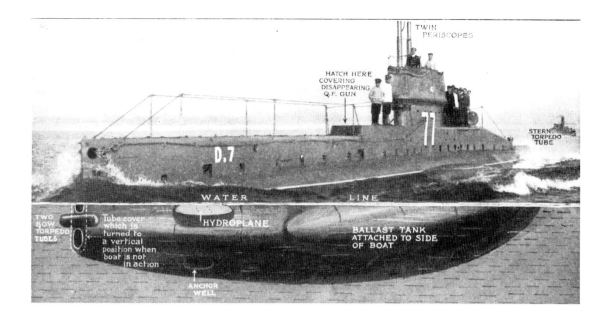

TWIN PERISCOPES

HATCH HERE COVERING DISAPPEARING Q.F. GUN

STERN TORPEDO TUBE

D.7

WATER LINE

TWO BOW TORPEDO TUBES

Tube cover which is turned to a vertical position when boat is not in action

HYDROPLANE

BALLAST TANK ATTACHED TO SIDE OF BOAT

ANCHOR WELL

Top: One of Britain's deadly mosquitoes of the ocean.

Right: Fixing an airship's propeller 2,000 feet above the sea.

Opposite: Throwing overboard all inflammable luxuries when a battleship is cleared for action.

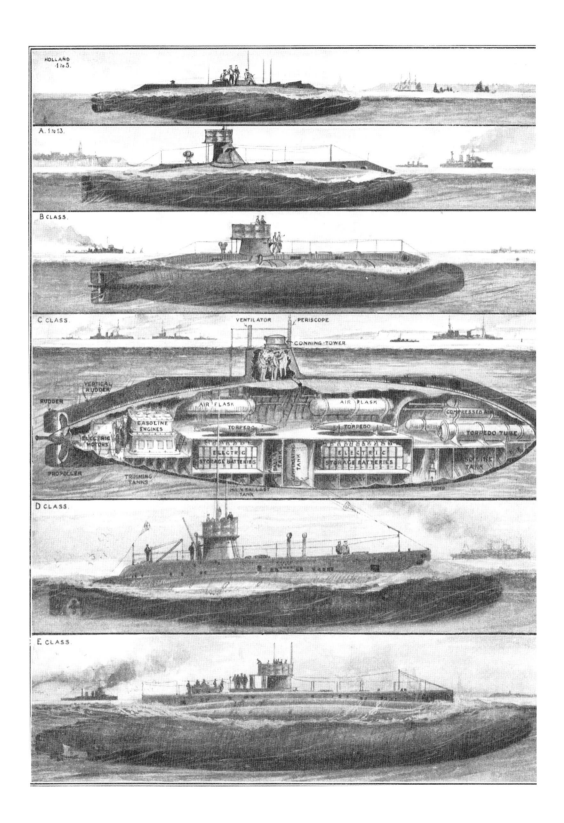

HOLLAND 1 to 5.

A. 1 to 13.

B CLASS.

C CLASS.

VENTILATOR   PERISCOPE

CONNING TOWER

VERTICAL RUDDER

RUDDER

AIR FLASK   AIR FLASK   COMPRESSED AIR

GASOLINE ENGINES   TORPEDO   TORPEDO   TORPEDO TUBE

ELECTRIC MOTORS

ELECTRIC STORAGE BATTERIES   ELECTRIC STORAGE BATTERIES

PROPELLER   TRIMMING TANKS   MAIN BALLAST TANK

D CLASS.

E CLASS.

Top: What the inside of a submarine is like.

Right: The marvellous 'eye' of the submarine.

Opposite: Graphic illustration of the development of the British submarine

British pluck shines in the hour of cruelest disaster.

Decoy torpedo-boat destroyers fleeing from a hostile cruiser in order to bring the latter within range of a waiting submarine's torpedos.

DECOYING DESTROYERS

A submarine resting on
the ocean bed.

"Sunk the lot." The famous exploit of Commander Cecil H. Fox who sent four German destroyers to the bottom.

German submarine rammed by the British destroyer *Badger* off the Belgian coast.

Above: Detecting a submarine beneath the sea.

Opposite: The First Lord with his two highest executive Officers.

Rescued by submarine off Heligoland.

Cheering the German submarine *U9*.

Scenes from the first naval battle off Heligoland.

The first cruiser squadron sighting the enemy

In port after the first naval battle – a scene off Harwich.

The bait that drew out the German ships of war which were destroyed in the battle of the Bight of Heligoland.

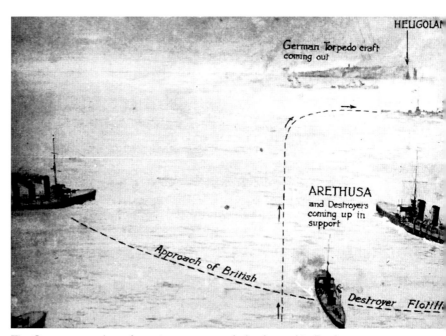

The German torpedo craft coming out to attack the decoy ship *Fearless* as the stratagem developed in the action off Heligoland.

GOLAND   FRISIAN ISLANDS

British submarines
returning to the
offshore as if disabled

ESS"
g to

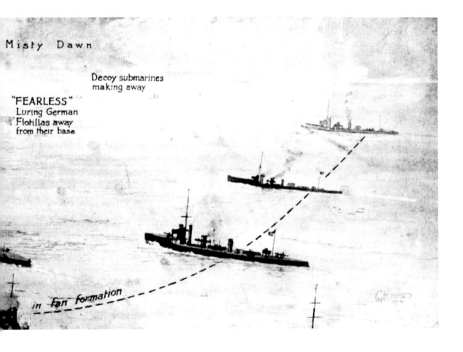

Misty Dawn

Decoy submarines
making away

"FEARLESS"
Luring German
Flotillas away
from their base

in fan formation

HELIGOLAND

3 German Cruisers

① ② ③

British & German destroyers in action

FEARLESS towing ARETHUSA

Air Light Cruiser Squadron

British chivalry: Rescuing German crews off Heligoland.

General impression of the Battle of Heligoland, showing the larger British ships waiting in the hope of a general sortie of the German Fleet. This diagrammatic representation shows the battle at its full height - the German cruisers and the British and German destroyers on the skyline; the disabled *Arethusa* being towed out of action by the *Fearless*; and the cruisers and the battle-cruisers of the British fleet waiting in the foreground in the expectation that the German battleships would come out to assist their cruisers and accept the challenge of battle. But the main German fleet preferred the inglorious security of the protection of their land forts.

The Arethusa in a circle of German naval attack.

Chapter 2

THE WAR IN THE NORTH SEA

The North Sea was the main theatre of the war for surface action. Immediately following the outbreak of war, the British Grand Fleet took position against the German High Seas Fleet. Britain's larger fleet could maintain a blockade of Germany, cutting it off from overseas trade and resources. As a result, Germany's fleet remained mostly in harbour behind their screen of mines, occasionally attempting to lure the British fleet into battle (one such attempt was the bombardment of Yarmouth and Lowestoft) in the hopes of weakening them enough to break the blockade or allow the High Seas Fleet to attack British shipping and trade. Britain strove to maintain the blockade and, if possible, to damage the German fleet enough to remove the threat to the islands and free the Grand Fleet for use elsewhere.

Major battles of the early part of the war included those at Heligoland Bight. The First Battle of Heligoland Bight was the first naval battle of the First World War, fought on 28 August 1914, between the United Kingdom and Germany. The battle took place in the south-eastern North Sea when the British attacked German patrols off the northwest German coast.

The German High Seas Fleet remained largely in safe harbours on the north German coast while the British Grand Fleet remained in the northern North Sea. Both sides engaged in long-distance sorties with cruisers and battlecruisers, and close reconnaissance of the area of sea near the German coast—the Heligoland Bight—by destroyer. The British devised a plan to ambush German destroyers on their daily patrols. A British fleet of 31 destroyers and two cruisers under Commodore Reginald Tyrwhitt and submarines commanded by Commodore Roger Keyes was dispatched. They were supported at longer range by an additional six light cruisers commanded by William Goodenough, and five battlecruisers commanded by Vice Admiral David Beatty.

Three German light cruisers and one destroyer were sunk. Three more light cruisers were damaged, 712 sailors killed, 530 injured and 336 taken prisoner. The British suffered one light cruiser and three destroyers damaged, 35 killed and 40 wounded. The battle was regarded as a great victory in Britain, where the returning ships were met by cheering crowds. Vice Admiral Beatty was regarded as the hero of Heligoland Bight , although he had taken little part in the action or planning of the raid, which was led by Commodore Tyrwhitt and conceived by himself and Keyes, who had persuaded the Admiralty to adopt it. However, the raid might have led to disaster had the additional forces under Beatty not been sent by Admiral John Jellicoe at the last minute.

The effect upon the German government and in particular the Kaiser was to restrict the freedom of action of the German fleet, instructing it to remain in port and avoid any contact with superior forces.

On 2 November 1914, Blücher—along with the battlecruisers *Moltke*, *Von der Tann*, and *Seydlitz*, and accompanied by four light cruisers, left the Jade Bight and steamed towards the English coast. The flotilla arrived off Great Yarmouth at daybreak the following morning and bombarded the port, while the light cruiser *Stralsund* laid a minefield. The British submarine HMS *D5* responded to the bombardment, but struck one of the mines laid by *Stralsund* and sank. Shortly thereafter, Hipper ordered his ships to turn back to German waters. On the way, a heavy fog covered the Heligoland Bight, so the ships were ordered to halt until visibility improved and they could safely navigate the defensive minefields. The armoured cruiser *Yorck* made a navigational error that led her into one of the German minefields. She struck two mines and quickly sank; only 127 men out of the crew of 629 were rescued.

British mine-layers at work in the North Sea.

A haul in the English Channel.

The British Battle Squadron at full speed in 'the Narrow Seas'

HMS *Cumberland*'s picket-boat in the Cameroon River.

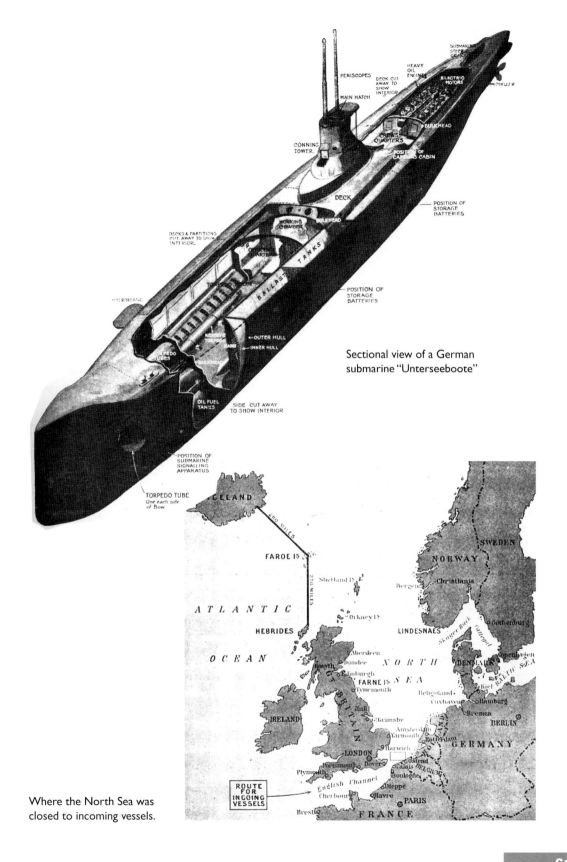

Sectional view of a German
submarine "Unterseeboote"

Where the North Sea was
closed to incoming vessels.

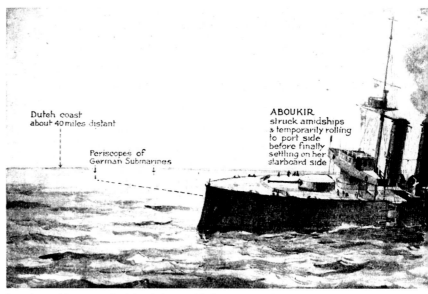

British naval losses in the North Sea on 22 September, 1914, when the
Aboukir, *Hogue* and *Cressy* were torpedoed by German submarines.
The *Aboukir*, the first of the three cruisers to be hit, was struck by a torpedo.

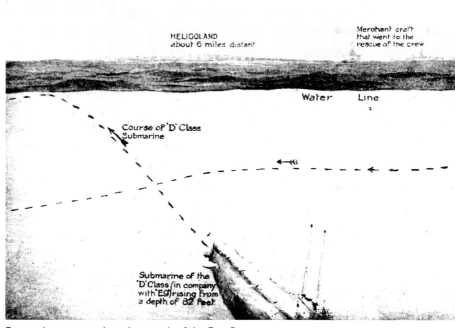

Enemy destroyer sunk at the mouth of the Ems River.

HOGUE
lowering
boats

CRESSY

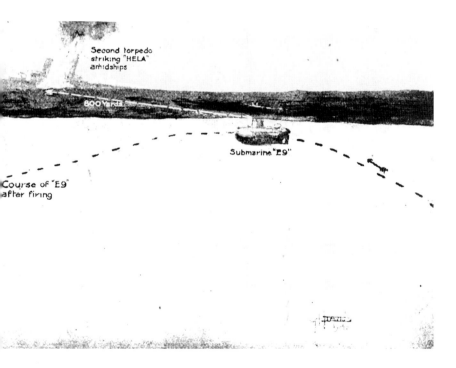

Second torpedo
striking "HELA"
amidships

800 Yards

Submarine "E9"

Course of "E9"
after firing

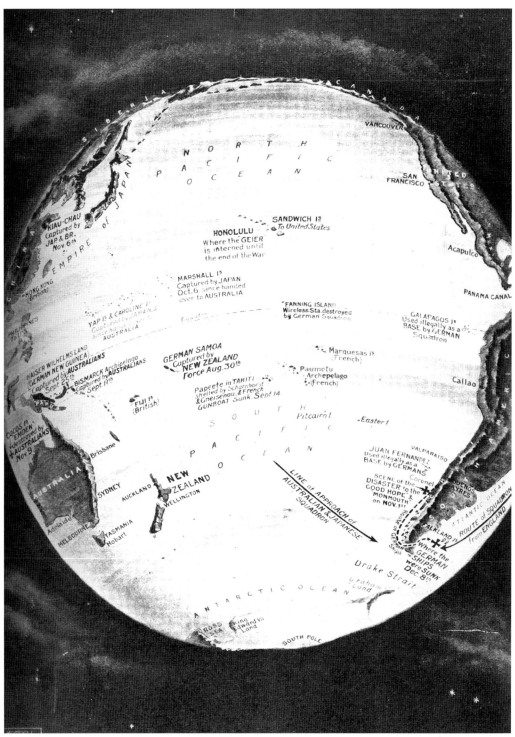

Where Germany lost her 'place in the sun'. Diagram showing how the Pax Britannica was secured in the waters of the Pacific.

Sinking of the Russian cruiser *Pallada* in the Baltic. When on patrol duty with a sister ship, the *Byan*, in the Baltic, the *Pallada* was struck by a torpedo from a German submarine and sent to the bottom so quickly that few of her crew of 568 officers and men escaped.

The Kaiser's grand objective. This admirable picture map of the Channel coast-line from Dunkirk to Bologne is the work of a German professor, and was published in Germany at the time when the Kaiser had ordered his impotent hordes to 'take Calais or die.' It shows at a glance how important to the German designs on England was the capture of Calais.

How the Russian Baltic fleet puts to sea in Winter.

How the British monitors evaded the German fire off the Belgian coast.

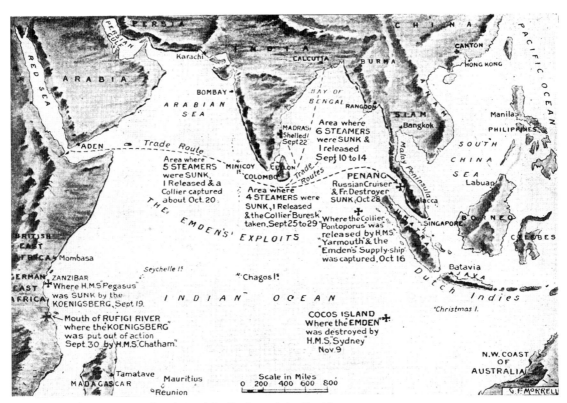

Map showing the cruisings and exploits of the *Emden* and the *Konisberg*.

The fight off the Falklands: How the *Glasgow* and *Cornwall* sank the *Leipzig*.

Above: Opening stage of the great battle off the Falklands. Left to right the *Glasgow*, *Invincible* and *Inflexible* engaging the *Scharnhorst* and *Gneisenau*, and the *Nurnberg*, *Leipzig* and *Dresden* in flight.

Below: Key plan of the naval action off Coronel in Chile.

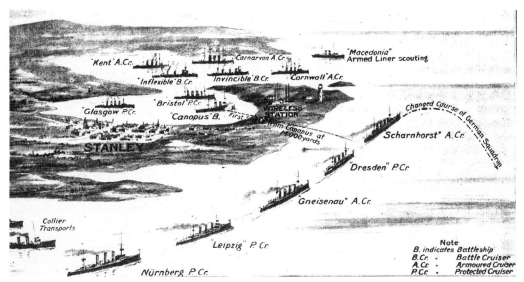

Above: The morning of Admiral Sturdee's victory.

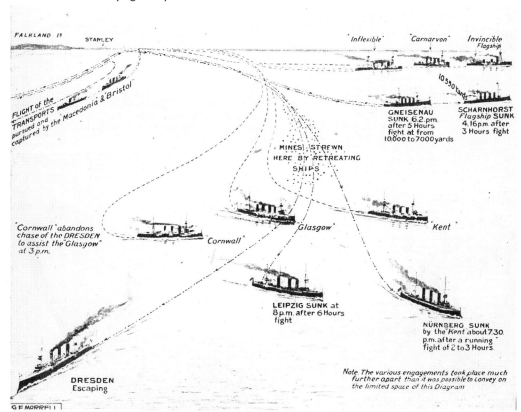

Below: Pursuit of the flying enemy cruisers.

Chapter 3

THE WAR EXTENDS

Admiral Friedrich von Ingenohl, commander of the German High Seas Fleet, decided that another raid on the English coast should be carried out in the hopes of luring a portion of the Grand Fleet into combat where it could be destroyed. However the British Naval Intelligence Room 40 began decrypting German signals, and on 14 December 1914, intercepted messages relating to the plan to bombard Scarborough. The exact details of the plan were unknown. On 15 December 1914, *Blücher*, *Moltke*, *Von der Tann*, the new battlecruiser *Derfflinger*, and *Seydlitz*, along with the light cruisers *Kolberg*, *Strassburg*, *Stralsund*, *Graudenz*, and two squadrons of torpedo boats left the Jade estuary. The ships sailed north past the island of Heligoland, until they reached the Horns Reef lighthouse, at which point the ships turned west towards Scarborough. Twelve hours after Hipper left the Jade, the High Seas Fleet, consisting of 14 dreadnoughts and eight pre-dreadnoughts and a screening force of two armoured cruisers, seven light cruisers, and 54 torpedo boats, departed to provide distant cover for the bombardment force.

Vice Admiral Beatty's four battlecruisers, supported by the 3rd Cruiser Squadron and the 1st Light Cruiser Squadron, along with the 2nd Battle Squadron's six dreadnoughts, were to ambush Hipper's battlecruisers.

On the night of 15/16 December, the main body of the High Seas Fleet encountered British destroyers. Fearing the prospect of a night time torpedo attack, Admiral Ingenohl ordered the ships to retreat. Hipper was unaware of Ingenohl's reversal, and so he continued with the bombardment. Upon reaching the British coast, Hipper's battlecruisers split into two groups. *Seydlitz*, *Moltke*, and *Blücher* went north to shell Hartlepool, while *Von der Tann* and *Derfflinger* went south to shell Scarborough and Whitby. Of the three towns, only Hartlepool was defended by coastal artillery batteries. During the bombardment of Hartlepool, *Seydlitz* was hit three times and *Blücher* was hit six times by the coastal battery. *Blücher* suffered minimal damage, but nine men were killed and another three were wounded. By 09:45 on the 16th, the two groups had reassembled, and they began to retreat eastward.

By this time, Beatty's battlecruisers were in position to block Hipper's chosen escape route, while other forces were en route to complete the encirclement. At 12:25, the light cruisers of the II Scouting Group began to pass through the British forces searching for Hipper. One of the cruisers in the 2nd Light Cruiser Squadron spotted *Stralsund* and signalled a report to Beatty. At 12:30, Beatty turned his battlecruisers towards the German ships. Beatty presumed that the German cruisers were the advance screen for Hipper's ships, but the battlecruisers were some 30 miles ahead. The 2nd Light Cruiser Squadron, which had been screening for Beatty's ships, detached to pursue the German cruisers, but a misinterpreted signal from the British battlecruisers sent them back to their screening positions. This confusion allowed the German light cruisers to escape and alerted Hipper to the location of the British battlecruisers. The German battlecruisers wheeled to the northeast of the British forces and made good their escape

In addition to the actions in the North Sea other naval engagements were taking place. A number of German ships stationed overseas at the start of the war engaged in raiding operations in poorly defended seas, such as SMS *Emden*, which raided into the Indian Ocean, sinking or capturing thirty Allied merchant ships and warships, bombarding Madras and Penang, and destroying a radio relay on the Cocos Islands before being sunk there by HMAS *Sydney*. Better known was the German East Asia Squadron, commanded by Admiral Graf Maximilian von Spee, who sailed across the Pacific, raiding Papeete and winning the Battle of Coronel before being defeated and mostly destroyed at the Battle of the Falkland Islands. The last remnants of Spee's squadron were interned at Chilean ports and destroyed at the Battle of Mas a Tierra.

Allied naval forces captured many of the isolated German colonies, with Samoa, Micronesia, Qingdao, German New Guinea, Togo, and Cameroon falling in the first year of the war. As Austria-Hungary refused to withdraw its cruiser SMS *Kaiserin Elisabeth* from the German naval base of Tsingtao, Japan declared war not only on Germany, but also on Austria-Hungary. The cruiser participated in the defence of Tsingtao where it was sunk in November 1914. Despite the loss of the last German cruiser in the Indian Ocean, SMS *Königsberg*, off the coast of German East Africa in July 1915, German East Africa held out in a long guerilla land campaign.

Scarborough and its environs.

Loss of HMS *Formidable* off Torbay: Fate of the boats which got away from the sinking battleship.

The German bombardment of Hartlepool. Shells falling on the battery at the end of the pier.

Shells from German warships bursting over Scarborough sea front. According to the *Berliner Lokal-Anzeiger* defenceless, pleasure-loving Scarborough is 'the most important on the East coast of England between the Humber and the Thames'. The *Berliner Tageblatt* also described Scarborough as being an important port.

Above and below: German artists view of the effect of 'frightfulness' at Scarborough.

HMS *Lion*, Vice-Admiral Beatty's flagship, going into action.

After the battle: The *Indomitable* towing the *Lion* back to port.

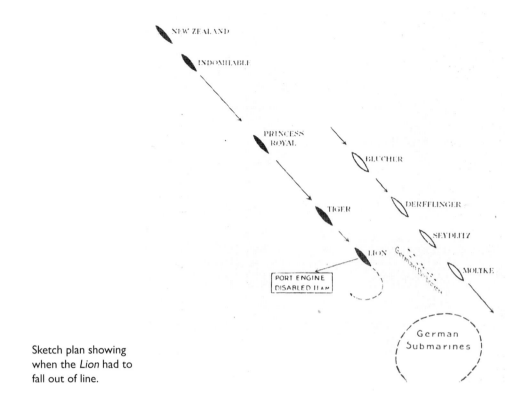

NEW ZEALAND

INDOMITABLE

PRINCESS ROYAL

BLUCHER

DERFFLINGER

TIGER

SEYDLITZ

LION *German Battle Cruisers*

MOLTKE

PORT ENGINE DISABLED 11 A.M.

German Submarines

Sketch plan showing when the *Lion* had to fall out of line.

Triumphs of marine engineering: A 200-ton crane lowering a boiler into a liner.

Sinking of the Turkish battleship *Messudiyeh* by submarine *B11*.

Zeppelin holding up a merchant vessel in the North Sea.

Outwitting the enemy: Thrilling incident of the air raid on Cuxhaven.

Map of the Dardanelles and Gallipoli Peninsula, specially drawn to illustrate the operations by land and water which began in the spring of 1915.

The sinking of HMS *Irresistible* during an attack on the forts at the
Narrows of the Dardanelles, March 18th, 1915.

British warship attacking the outer forts of the Dardanelles.

Pirate submarine *U12* rammed by the British destroyer *Arial* and fired on by HMS *Attack*, March 10th 1915.
Out of the submarine's crew of 28 the number saved was ten.

The loss of the French cruiser
Leon Gambetta, torpedoed in he
strait of Otranto 1915.

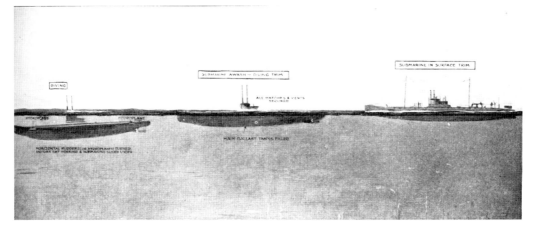

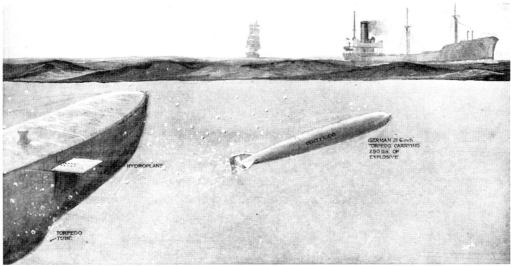

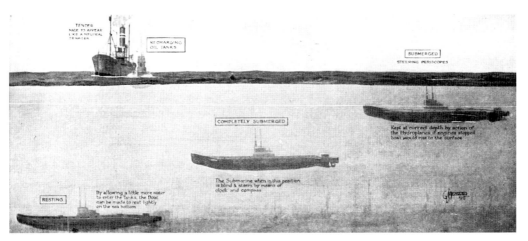

How the German submarine went about its deadly work.
Top: First stage – from surface trim to diving
Middle: Second stage – Discharging a torpedo while submerged.
Bottom: Third stage – submerged after sinking its prey.

FUNNEL
DAMAGED
BOAT DECK

PROMENADE DECK

SHELTER DECK

← Dotted line →
represents
approximate
height of water
& debris thrown
up by the explosion

Approximate size
of vast hole caused
by Torpedo.

Torpedo

← Area affected (Rivets started Etc) →

Approximate view of the cavernous hole through which the sea rushed when the *Lusitania* was torpedoed by the German submarine *U21* off the Irish Coast on 7 May 1915.

Rescue work after the disappearance of the *Lusitania*. It was announced in June 1915, that the Kaiser had conferred on Captain-Lieutenant Hersing commander of the *U21*, the Order "Pour le Merite," in recognition of his "gallant act" in torpedoing the *Lusitania*. The same submarine sank the *Pathfinder* in September, 1914.

Somewhere amid the Northern mists. British naval officer's impression of the quarter-deck of one of the ships of the Grand Fleet at night after a snowfall.

The sinking of the German submarine *U8* off Dover, 5 March, 1915.

HMS *Spitfire* torpedoing a German Cruiser on the night of 31 May 1916.

A perilous "fish" out of water. Section of a German sea-mine being placed on the Horse Guards Parade.

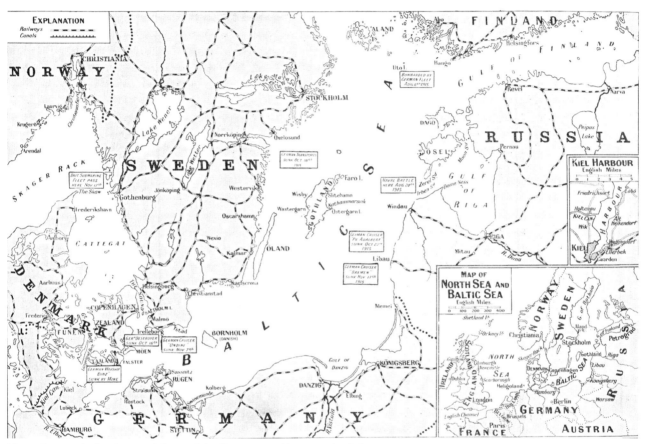

Map indicating the localities and dates of the German naval losses in the Baltic.

Another victim of the U Pirates. White Star liner *Arabic*, outward bound for New York, sinking off Kinsale on 19 August, 1915, with a loss of 32 lives. This photograph was secured by Professor Still, of Purdue University, USA, as the lifeboat was leaving the vessel's side.

Commander Max Kennedy Horton, RN, DSO, one of Britain's heroes of the Baltic.

Hide and seek in the Baltic: Zeppelin flies over the British submarine in the stormy sea.

Blockade incident: British destroyer overhauls a neutral ship to search for contraband.

A battle of four elements: British monitors shell German land batteries near Nieuport.

The Admiral's eyes and ears: Dramatic impression of British destroyers on the alert.

Deep sea fishing for men. Having sunk an enemy vessel, the British sailors set to work to save the crew. One hauled in the lifeline, while a second helped the foe aboard.

Preserving the British tradition at sea. A German watching his comrades in the sea while his captors are busily engaged in rescue work forward.

"Periscope astern to Starboard!" A moment of suspense aboard a British destroyer patrolling the North Sea. Out of a choppy sea there suddenly appeared a periscope. With a hiss of foam astern, the destroyer swung round – and then a gleam of sunlight revealed the top of a floating spar, riding upright in the water!

The "eye" of a submarine: surface view from beneath the sea. A submarine's field of vision through the periscope, with marks denoting measurements by which the distance of the objective can be gauged. Here a German warship is seen, 'hull down' in a rough sea at a distance of a few hundred yards.

The man behind the periscope, on whose keenness of eye depends the safety of the submarine. In these illustrations by a naval officer, the 'lookout' man is taking the measure of an enemy vessel, prior to the launching of a torpedo.

After a brush with the Turks near the Tigris. British troops re-embarking on board one of our ships on the River Tigris after a fight with the Turks in Mesopotamia, along the desert way to Bagdad. Note the machine-guns at the side.

Map of the Aegean Sea, one of the principal areas of allied and enemy submarine activity in 1915-1916.

Map of Gallipoli indicating the landing places from Seddul Bahr to Sulva.

'Dhobing' in the fleet: wash-clothes day on board a British patrol. Keeping up their reputation as clean fighters. Jack Tars washing clothes on a British monitor in the North Sea, an occupation known as 'dhobing'.

Lifeboatman 'doing their bit.' The use of mines and the absence of navigation lights at sea resulted in a number of wrecks round British coasts, augmenting the duties of lifeboatman. This illustration shows the Spurn lifeboat on an errand of mercy, supported by a railway company's tug.

German air-raiders bombing Salonika. An anti-aircraft gun on a British warship firing at the three enemy aeroplanes which raided Salonika and dropped about thirty bombs, on the morning of 30 December, 1915. This flagrant act of war on Greek soil was followed by the arrest of the Consuls of Germany, Austria, Turkey and Bulgaria, who the same evening, were conveyed on board a French warship.

On the alert for the furtive foe: Scene in a submerged British submarine.

Sentinels of he Grand Fleet: Patrol boat overhauling suspected blockade-runner.

Courage and skill overcome mine peril: Exploding infernal
machines bought to the surface by trawlers.

Left: Taking possession of the prize. British soldiers aboard the *UC5*. The German commander attempted to destroy the craft with bombs, which exploded ineffectually after the crew had abandoned it.

Below: British monitors in action with the enemy batteries ashore. Monitors did excellent work not only in the Dardanelles, but also off the Belgian coast, where they constantly harassed the German right flank. The two shown here were engaging the enemy at long range, while the crews of their small guns stood by to repel possible submarine attacks.

SS *Avocet* attacked by three German aeroplanes. The SS *Avocet*, when off the West Hinder lightship, 30 October, 1915, was attacked by three aeroplanes, which bombed her heavily for half an hour. So well was she handled that no bomb hit her. Before flying off, one aeroplane hit her with a machine gun, but wounded none of the crew.

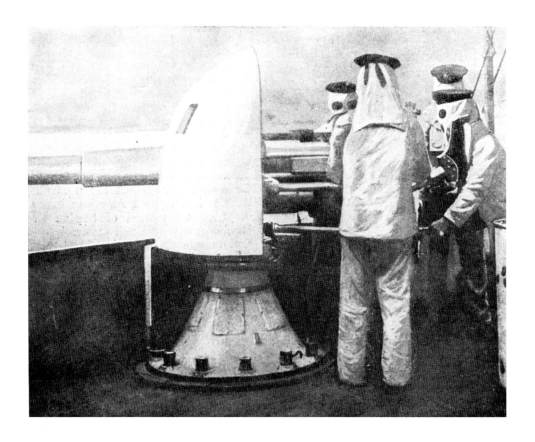

Above: Masqueraders of the
Adriatic. Weird appearance of
Austrian naval gunners equipped
with respirators against the effect
of poison gas generated by the
explosion of their shells.

Left: On dangerous duty on the
Dardanelles. Two naval officers
fishing a mine from the Dardanelles,
apparently unconcerned that the
machine might explode at any
moment.

Right: A released mine rising from the sea bed, whilst its carrier-cage remains stationary to anchor the machine.

DETONATORS

VALVE from which safety pin has automatically been withdrawn, rendering Detonators active

MINE RISING

HYDROSTATIC VALVE

HINGED GUIDES FALLING FLAT to anchor & prevent mine from capsizing

SAFETY PIN released from valve

MINE SUPPORT

DRUM

SINKER

Below: How a German submarine mine-layer worked in the high seas. Sectional drawing of the captured German submarine mine layer *UC5*, indicating the method of sowing mines in the track of hostile shipping. One of the most interesting features of the *UC5* was the jumping wire, to facilitate the submarine's passage through net defences and entanglements under water.

PERISCOPE

HATCH

STEERING WHEEL

BINNACLE

JUMPING WIRE FOR NEGOTIATING NET DEFENCES

CONNING TOWER

UC 5

DIESEL ENGINES

ELECTRIC MOTORS

LOCKERS ETC

LIVING COMPARTMENT

NAVIGATING COMPARTMENT

STORAGE TANKS CYLINDERS, ETC

STORES

MINE LAYING COMPARTMENT

CATCH CONNECTED TO LEVER IN CONNING TOWER FOR RELEASING MINES

MINE RELEASED

SUPERSTRUCTURE

POSITION OF GUN

6 MINE CHUTES

CHUTE ENCLOSING CHUTES

BOWS

EXTERIOR OF CHUTE

FLUKE

HYDROPLANE

Off Schleswig: British destroyers and seaplanes in action during a storm, 25 March, 1916.

Off Jutland: Lucky shot destroys German torpedo and saves a British warship.

Daylight signalling in the British Navy: Heliographing a long distance message by the aid of a searchlight.

Above: Rescue in sight: Soldiers aboard one of the *Ivernia*'s rafts watching an approaching patrol.

Below: Coolness and courage: Troops on the *Ivernia* before taking to the boats.

Swamped by breakers: One of the boats from the transport *Ivernia*, torpedoed 1 January, 1917.

Signalling to the great: 'Go slowly for the sake of the small.'

Right: Fishing for mines: a catch. Crew of a German mine-sweeper watching a mine rising to the surface. Trawling for mines was most dangerous work, requiring great vigilance and courage. Mines brought up by the cables were exploded by rifle fire.

Left: The crew of a U-boat on deck doing various small repairs necessitated by mishaps during a spell of dirty weather.

Below: How the enemy depicted an alleged German success. German cruiser out on patrol destroying an English mine-layer. This illustration is produced from a German newspaper, and may be founded on fact. No enemy surface mine-layers ventured near the English coast, but British mine-layers had to operate near German waters.

America's coastal defences: Powerful mortar in action.

An armed merchantman: A Falmouth packet, about 1790, beating off an enemy near the Manacles.

The wrecked zeppelin: A German airship brought down in the channel.

British foodships successfully convoyed by seaplanes in clear weather when U-boats were easier to see.